Januar‹

To LaVor

May you enjoy these
memories of my dad.
Love, Ruth Stoneman

REMEMBERING
SEVEN PROPHETS

Gordon B. Hinckley

REMEMBERING SEVEN PROPHETS

Gordon B. Hinckley

MEMORIES OF FRANCIS M. GIBBONS
AS TOLD TO DANIEL BAY GIBBONS

Sixteen Stones Press

HOLLADAY, UTAH

Book layout, typography, and cover design ©2015 by Julie G. Gibbons. Photo credits: all cover photographs from the private collection of Francis M. Gibbons, used by permission. Sixteen Stones Press logo design by Marina Telezar.

Sixteen Stones Press
Publisher website: www.sixteenstonespress.com

Gordon B. Hinckley
(Remembering Seven Prophets, Book 6)
by Daniel Bay Gibbons

Paperback ISBN 978-1-942640-16-5
eBook ISBN 978-1-942640-17-2

TABLE OF CONTENTS

REMEMBERING SEVEN PROPHETS

This collection of reminiscences about the life of President Gordon B. Hinckley, the fifteenth President of The Church of Jesus Christ of Latter-day Saints is part of a larger work entitled *Remembering Seven Prophets*. This work is the fruit of more than eighty hours of interviews I conducted with my father, Francis M. Gibbons, between the years 2001 to 2011, and then another dozen hours of interviews conducted between July and December of 2014 following my return from presiding over the Russia Novosibirsk Mission of the Church.

"A Plutarch to the Presidents of the Church"

Now in his ninety-fifth year, Francis M. Gibbons is perhaps the greatest student on the lives of the Presidents of the Church in this dispensation. He has two unique qualifications to speak and write about the Prophets.

First, over the past forty-five years, my father has become "a Plutarch to the Presidents of the Church." This unusual phrase has reference to Plutarch, the ancient Greek writer, who became the most famous biographer in history, the "Father of Biography." Many years ago my father shared with my mother his special aspiration to become "a Plutarch to the Presidents of the Church, and through their lives to write the history of the Church." If any man or woman deserves the title "Plutarch to the Presidents of the Church," it is my father, Francis M. Gibbons. Over the past four decades he has become by far the most prolific writer of biographies of the Presidents of the Church, writing a full-length biography of every Prophet from Joseph Smith to Gordon B. Hinckley. Dad's biographies of the Prophets have been very popular, selling many hundreds of thousands of copies. Thirteen of his presidential biographies have been included in Brigham Young University's list of "Sixty Significant Mormon Biographies." He has truly become "a Plutarch to the Presidents of the Church."

"A Scribe to the Prophets"

Second, my father has been a personal witness and observer of the character of the last seven Presidents of the Church:

Presidents Joseph Fielding Smith, Harold B. Lee, Spencer W. Kimball, Ezra Taft Benson, Howard W. Hunter, Gordon B. Hinckley, and Thomas S. Monson. He knew these men personally. He worked with them. While serving from 1970 to 1986 as the secretary to the First Presidency and later as a member of the Seventy, Dad associated with them on a daily basis. He was a "Scribe to the Prophets," as were William Clayton, Wilford Woodruff, Joseph F. Smith, William F. Gibbons, Joseph Anderson, and others before him.

"I am their witness"

When Dad was sustained as a General Authority in April of 1986, after many years serving as the faithful scribe for the Presidents of the Church, he said:

> The Church is led by prophets, seers, and revelators. I am their witness. I testify that they are honorable, upright, dedicated men of integrity, committed to teaching the principles of the gospel, who strive with all of their might to prepare a people ready for the return of the head of the Church, Jesus Christ, at His second coming.

This work, *Remembering Seven Prophets*, shares many unique stories, anecdotes, insights, and testimonies about the last seven Presidents of the Church, which are nowhere else available.

I offer this work for the enlightenment and inspiration of the reader and as a tribute to the memory of the seven Presidents of the Church featured in these pages. I love and honor these great men, and add my witness to that of my father that they were and are Prophets of God!

Daniel Bay Gibbons
August 4, 2015
Holladay, Utah

Chronology of the Life of President Gordon B. Hinckley

June 23, 1910
Gordon Bitner Hinckley is born in Salt Lake City, Utah, to Bryant S. Hinckley and Ada Bitner Hinckley.

June 1928
President Gordon B. Hinckley graduates from LDS High School

November 9, 1930
President Gordon B. Hinckley's mother, Ada Bitner Hinckley, dies.

June 1932
President Gordon B. Hinckley graduates from the University of Utah.

1933 to 1935
President Gordon B. Hinckley serves as a full-time missionary in England.

August 1935
President Gordon B. Hinckley, upon his return from his mission, is hired as the executive

secretary of the Church Radio, Publicity, and Mission Literature Committee.

April 29, 1937
President Gordon B. Hinckley marries Marjorie Pay.

1937 to 1946
President Gordon B. Hinckley serves on the Sunday School General Board.

May 1941
President Gordon B. Hinckley completes construction on a new home in East Millcreek.

January 1945
President Gordon B. Hinckley moves his family to Denver, where he works for the Denver and Rio Grande Railroad.

Fall of 1945
President Gordon B. Hinckley moves his family back to Salt Lake City.

November 14, 1948
President Gordon B. Hinckley is called as first counselor in the East Millcreek Stake presidency.

October 28, 1956
President Gordon B. Hinckley is called as president of the East Millcreek Stake.

April 6, 1958
President Gordon B. Hinckley is called as an Assistant to the Quorum of the Twelve.

June 5, 1961
President Gordon B. Hinckley's father, Bryant S. Hinckley, dies.

September 30, 1961
President Gordon B. Hinckley is called and sustained as a member of the Quorum of the Twelve.

September 1972
President Gordon B. Hinckley travels to the Holy Land with President Harold B. Lee.

July 15, 1981
President Gordon B. Hinckley is called as an additional counselor in the First Presidency by President Spencer W. Kimball.

May 6, 1982
President Gordon B. Hinckley is admitted to the hospital for the first time in his life.

November 27, 1982
President N. Eldon Tanner passes away.

December 2, 1982
President Gordon B. Hinckley is set apart as second counselor in the First Presidency.

November 10, 1985
President Gordon B. Hinckley is set apart as first counselor in the First Presidency under President Ezra Taft Benson.

June 5, 1994
President Gordon B. Hinckley is set apart as first counselor to President Howard W. Hunter.

March 12, 1995
President Gordon B. Hinckley is ordained and set apart as the fifteenth President of the Church.

January 27, 2008

President Gordon B. Hinckley dies in Salt Lake City at the age of 97.

"THE SON AND GRANDSON OF STAKE PRESIDENTS"

My sense is much of President Hinckley's self confidence comes from his father's influence and a heritage rich in Church service. He was the son and grandson of stake presidents. His father, Bryant S. Hinckley, was the president of the Liberty Stake for many years, a well-known speaker and writer, and a confidant of President Heber J. Grant and other General Authorities. Bryant S. Hinckley was the son of Ira Hinckley, who also was a stake president, and the brother of Elder Alonzo A. Hinckley, who was a stake president and later a member of the Twelve. Another of Bryant's brothers, Arza Hinckley, also served as a stake president. And before President Hinckley was called as a General Authority, he also served as a stake president. Interestingly, both of President Hinckley's sons have served as stake presidents, putting an exclamation mark upon the rich heritage of significant Church service in the Hinckley family. From his youth, therefore, Gordon B. Hinckley knew that he came from a line of solid Mormon leaders who had inspired the confidence of men in high places. The Hinckley family were all men and women of intelligence and substance who were his exemplars and role models. Young Gordon B. Hinckley admired them and sought to emulate them. And it is apparent he was amenable to their instruction and example. A notable example of this occurred shortly after Gordon entered the mission field. He was not having much success and was discouraged. He wrote home and told his father he was wasting his time and the father's money and that he ought to go home. The father answered in a brief letter, which said in substance: "Dear Gordon. I have received and read your letter. Forget yourself and go to work." Love, Father." I heard President Hinckley tell this story to a group of missionaries in Quito, Ecuador. He said it was the best advice he had ever received and that he could think of no better advice than this to pass on to the missionaries.

"THE NAME HINCKLEY WILL BECOME KNOWN AMONG ALL NATIONS"

President Hinckley always spoke with deep respect and of his father, Bryant S. Hinckley. I first sensed this when I took a long walk with President Hinckley in Fillmore, Utah, in the fall of 1975. We were en route to the rededication of the St. George Temple, traveling in a large bus with most of the General Authorities and their wives, and we stopped in Fillmore for lunch and a rest. President Hinckley, knowing that I loved to walk, suggested that the two of us take a long walk together to stretch our legs. This was a rare experience for me, as President Hinckley was in an expansive mood and spoke at great length about his family heritage, which has deep connections with Fillmore and Millard County.

As we walked that day, President Hinckley told me that his grandfather was the first stake president there in Fillmore, having first founded Cove Fort, in the nearby mountains. President Hinckley also talked much about his father, Bryant S. Hinckley, and his uncle, Elder Alonzo A. Hinckley. His father, Bryant, was a very well-known man in the Church, a writer, and the president of the Liberty Stake in the Salt Lake Valley. The brother, Alonzo, was less well known as a young man.

Alonzo Hinckley was also called as a stake president, like his father and brother, serving in the Deseret Stake, which included the western half of Millard County. President Hinckley told me that shortly after his Uncle Alonzo was sustained as stake president, a Brother Ashman who was then the stake patriarch came to him and said that he felt impressed to give Alonzo Hinckley a patriarchal blessing. Among other things, the patriarch told Brother Hinckley that if he would continue with the same zeal he then manifested, he would one day serve as a member of the Quorum of Twelve and that "the name Hinckley will become known among all nations."

President Hinckley said that his uncle received this special blessing in about 1912. More than two decades later, in 1934, Alonzo was indeed called to the Quorum of the Twelve, fulfilling the first promise uttered in the blessing by Patriarch Ashman. The fulfillment of the second promise, however, was not so clearly fulfilled, as Alonzo A.

Hinckley only served in the Twelve for two years, dying in 1936. Because of the brevity of his apostolic service, he was not well known even in his own lifetime, and today his name is hardly a footnote in the consciousness of the Latter-day Saints.

It is interesting to note that Elder Alonzo A. Hinckley's blessing never promised that *he* would become well known, only that *the name Hinckley* would become known among all nations.

For many years during the 1960s and 1970s my sons, Mark and Daniel, and I were assigned as the home teachers for Angie Hinckley Solomon and her family in the Yalecrest Ward in Salt Lake City. Angie was a daughter of Elder Alonzo A. Hinckley, and on one or two occasions she showed me the blessing given to her father, which President Hinckley alluded to during our walk together in Fillmore. It was Angie's feeling that her cousin, Gordon B. Hinckley, then a newly called member of the Twelve, would one day become the means of fulfilling that part of the blessing about the Hinckley name becoming known throughout the world.

That promise, uttered in 1912 by a patriarch in an obscure stake in the Church, has surely come to pass through the great service of Alonzo A. Hinckley's nephew, President Gordon B. Hinckley.

"THE EXAMPLE OF ROBERT LOUIS STEVENSON"

President Hinckley's father was a well-known writer of religious works, including biographies and works of Church history. Growing up in such a home., President Hinckley was well trained scholastically and in Church doctrine and procedure. He graduated from the University of Utah in English and English literature before serving his mission in England. He apparently did very well in his studies. At least the skill he displayed as a young missionary in both writing. and speaking the English language strongly imply this. His bent in this direction was influenced by his father who was an eloquent man and highly literate. During his university years, these qualities pointed Gordon B. Hinckley toward a career as a professional writer. President Hinckley told me once that as a young man he aspired to become a writer, and that he had gone so far as to lay plans to spend a year or so on a South Sea Island where he could study and write about the native culture. He told me that he was influenced by the example of Robert Louis Stevenson.

"WHEN HE WAS ELEVEN HE RECEIVED A PATRIARCHAL BLESSING"

President Hinckley told me that when he was eleven he received a patriarchal blessing in which he was told that he would preach and bear testimony in the nations of the earth. After his mission in Great Britain, he and Elder G. Homer Durham toured in Europe together, and in the process he had the opportunity to preach at meetings in both Germany and France. He felt afterward that since he had spoken in four different countries—the United States, England, Germany and France—this part of his patriarchal blessing had been completely fulfilled. Little did he know what was in store for him down the road. Since then, of course, he visited and spoke in most of the nations of the earth except for Tibet, Mongolia, and a few other nations in Africa and Eastern Europe.

"CLOSE ASSOCIATION WITH TWO APOSTLES"

Aside from his association with his great father, President Hinckley's first real Church training occurred in the mission field. While serving in England., he worked at mission headquarters, where he was on the staff of the *Millennial Star.* This brought him into close association with two Apostles, who served successively as President of the European Mission: Elder John A. Widtsoe and later Elder Joseph F. Merrill. From these two Apostles young Gordon gained important insight into the apostolic calling and Church administrative skills.

Among the great blessings of President Hinckley's mission was the beginning of his lifelong friendship with two of his missionary companions, Elder G. Homer Durham and Elder Richard L. Evans. Many years ago I heard Elder Widtsoe comment that the fame and influence of most great men depended upon the existence of devoted and able disciples. Such was the case with Joseph Smith. I think that if Elder Widtsoe ever occupies a place of commanding importance in Church history, it will be through his "disciples" who were his missionaries while he presided in Great Britain, including Gordon B. Hinckley, Richard L. Evans, and G. Homer Durham. Elder Evans, of course, served in the Quorum of the Twelve and Elder Durham in the Seventy.

After his mission, Elder Durham married the daughter of Elder John A. Widtsoe, who had been his mission president.

"President Grant told him, 'We will give you 15 minutes'"

In 1973, President Hinckley and I had a long conversation as we sat together on a flight from Munich to Frankfurt, Germany, during which he told me about some significant events which occurred at the conclusion of his mission to England. He told me that as he worked on the staff of the *Millennial Star,* he had become very close to Elder Joseph F. Merrill of the Twelve, who was then the president of the European Mission. Elder Merrill relied heavily upon President Hinckley, and in fact wrote to the First Presidency requesting that Gordon B. Hinckley's mission be extended for an additional six months. This request was turned down by the Brethren in Salt Lake City, and President Hinckley told me that Elder Merrill was very upset. In anger and with great emphasis, the Apostle told the young missionary, "The Brethren just don't understand our situation. I want you to explain it to them when you return home." He then wrote back personally to President Heber J. Grant, asking that young Elder Gordon B.

Hinckley be permitted to visit with the First Presidency when he returned home to Salt Lake City from England.

President Hinckley told me that when he went in to keep this specially arranged appointment with the First Presidency, President Grant told him, "We will give you 15 minutes." However, as the discussion proceeded, the Brethren asked him a number of questions, and Elder Hinckley remained with them for an hour and a half.

Shortly following this interview, President David O. McKay called President Hinckley and invited him to come to his office for an interview. At that time he called the young Elder Hinckley to become the secretary to a newly formed committee comprised of six members of the Twelve and chaired by President Stephen L. Richards. The committee was organized to explore ways to expand the outreach of the Church using not only print media, but radio and film.

President Hinckley obviously made quite an impression on the Brethren, as their contacts with him resulted almost immediately in his employment as a member of the Church administrative staff. The interesting thing is that except for a short interval during World War II when he was employed by the railroad, President Hinckley was continuously at Church headquarters from the time of his mission until his death at age 97, serving either on the staff or as a General Authority. President Hinckley ultimately worked at Church headquarters for nearly seventy-five years!

"SOMEDAY I'M GOING TO RUN THIS PLACE"

President Hinckley was searching for a job during the brief interval between his return home from his mission and his employment with the committee chaired by President McKay. Because of his love of literature and his boyhood aspirations to become a writer, he decided to try to get a job with the *Deseret News*. He made an appointment to visit with Samuel O. Bennion, general manager of the *News*, and asked him for a job. Brother Bennion was also serving at the time as a member of the First Council of the Seventy. President Hinckley told me that Brother Bennion, who was then a member of the First Council of Seventy, was quite brusque with him and turned him down cold. Moreover, he told President Hinckley that even if there were an opening, which there was not, there were others far better qualified than young Gordon B. Hinckley who would be given preference.

President Hinckley told me that as he left the interview with Samuel O. Bennion, he said to himself, "That's alright. Some day I'm going to run this place."

Years down the road, President Hinckley became the chairman of the board of the Deseret News. He did, indeed, run the *Deseret News*. This experience with Elder Bennion is very revealing of President Hinckley's character. Most young men would have been overawed by this man who was both the head of the *Deseret News* and also a General Authority of the Church. Moreover, to be turned down in this brusque way and to be told there were others better qualified than he would have been deflating and calculated to cause feelings of inferiority. But instead of leaving low and downhearted, this young man was positive and upbeat and not only confident of his future, but confident he one day would head the company which had just so summarily turned him away.

This experience reveals the supreme self-assurance that characterized President Hinckley's entire life and ministry.

"HE WAS THE WORKHORSE"

From the time of his return home from his mission in 1935 until his call as a General Authority in 1959, President Gordon B. Hinckley was employed. in various capacities at Church headquarters. His work on the staff was in three areas—Radio and Publicity, Temples, and Missionary Work.

President Hinckley's first assignment at Church headquarters was to become the secretary to the newly formed Radio and Publicity Committee, comprised of six members of the Twelve and chaired by Elder Stephen L. Richards. According to President Hinckley this committee had responsibility for all the radio and other public communications for the Church.

President Hinckley was paid a salary of $65.00 per month and supplemented that with $35.00 he received for teaching Seminary. He was the workhorse for the Committee—preparing scripts, editing, preparing and supervising their budget, etc. Later, after he had proven himself, he was asked by President J. Reuben Clark, President

Stephen L. Richards, and others to edit their radio, conference, and other talks.

Interestingly, I first met Gordon B. Hinckley in 1942 while he was still serving as the Secretary of the Church Radio and Publicity Committee. At the time, I was in the mission home in Salt Lake City, preparing to go to the Southern States Mission. At that time the missionaries were housed in several old two-story homes north of the Beehive House on the west side of State Street. Brother Hinckley was among those who came to instruct the missionaries. He was then only thirty-one years old. The impression that has stayed with me over the years was that of an able younger man who gave us good tips about how to obtain free airtime at radio stations to present our message. He seemed to be very self-confident and to know his subject. But I did not detect in this young Gordon B. Hinckley the surpassing eloquence he showed later. It could be I was not then tuned in to eloquence.

"PRESIDENT LEE SAW WHAT WAS AHEAD FOR HIM"

It was obvious to me from the time I became associated with the First Presidency that a strong bond existed between President Harold B. Lee and President Gordon B. Hinckley. It extended back to the days when they were both staff employees of the Church. President Hinckley began his work with the Radio and Publicity Committee in 1935, which was only a year before President Harold B. Lee was employed by the Church as the general manager of the newly formed Welfare Department of the Church. In that period, President Hinckley and President Lee had offices side by side on the second floor of the Administration building, and from that association formed the friendship which persisted for nearly forty years, until President Lee's death in 1973.

Also, it was President Lee who called President Hinckley as a stake president. President Lee later told President Hinckley that when he set him apart as a stake president, President Lee "saw what was ahead for him."

"THE LAND OF MIRACLES"

In the early 1980s, I had a lengthy conversation with President Hinckley about his special relationship with President Harold B. Lee. Shortly after President Lee was sustained as the President of the Church in July of 1972, he and President Hinckley and their wives went on a trip together that took them to Italy, Greece, and the Holy Land. At Jerusalem, President Lee, who had been having respiratory problems, took ill with heavy congestion in his lungs. Concerned about him, Sister Lee asked President Hinckley to administer to him. He in turn invited Ted Cannon (who was then serving as the mission president in Switzerland with jurisdiction over Jerusalem) to assist him. Brother Cannon anointed and President Hinckley sealed.

Later that night, President Hinckley said he heard loud coughing from President Lee's adjoining room, which continued for some time and then stopped. The next morning at breakfast when the Cannons were present, President Lee said nothing. But the following day, after the Cannons had left, President Lee said at breakfast, "I guess we have had to come to the land of miracles to see miracles in our own lives." He then explained that some time after President Hinckley's priesthood administration, the Prophet was taken ill and so seriously that he felt he was going to die. Finally, he said, he coughed up a large clot of blood and that the coughing then stopped. (It apparently was a similar attack that took President Lee's life only about sixteen months later).

President Hinckley told me that he later prepared a narrative of this unusual trip with the Prophet, based upon his journal, which he titled "A Trip to Remember" and had it bound in leather as a gift for President and Sister Lee.

There was one final journey that President Hinckley took with the Prophet before his death. In 1973, following the Munich Conference, Presidents Lee and Hinckley and their wives took a trip to Florence, Vienna, and through Northern Europe. On this trip, as well as the earlier one to the Holy Land, President Hinckley made all the travel arrangements for the four of them, there being no security personnel, doctors etc. nor travel agents, as is now the case when the President of the Church travels abroad. It was like a senior companion travelling with a junior companion with their wives along. Judging from his comments and tone, I inferred President Hinckley still felt that way toward President Lee—that he was like a senior companion—a feeling I also share.

"Conciliation and negotiation"

Another assignment that President Hinckley performed during these early years at Church headquarters was to work with President Stephen L. Richards in supervising the missionary work. One particularly thorny assignment involved the negotiation of draft deferments for LDS missionaries. President Hinckley told me that the policy followed by President Richards in this sensitive issue was always one of conciliation and negotiation. At the outset, Elder Hinckley told President Richards that the Brethren really needed a lawyer in the position they wanted Elder Hinckley to fill. President Richards' response to Gordon B. Hinckley was, "I'm a lawyer, and I don't want another one involved in this delicate matter. Another lawyer would want to fight and litigate this issue, and it is one that cannot be resolved that way."

President Richards' philosophy of conciliation and negotiation prevailed despite one instance when it appeared that President David O. McKay was determined to follow another course. A missionary who had been out for 19 months had been ordered by his local draft board to report for duty immediately. The anguished parents came to President McKay for help, and he invited President Richards and Elder Hinckley to join them. President Hinckley told me that during the emotional conversation with this family, President McKay said, bringing his fists down on the desk, "They shall not have him! We shall fight this to the very last, even if it consumes all the resources of the Church!" When the Prophet asked President Richards to comment, he asked: "But what if we should lose the case, President? Then our whole missionary effort would be frustrated." President McKay ultimately yielded and the policy of conciliation continued.

"WHAT WE WANT TO DO IS TO COMPOSE THIS MATTER"

Based upon many private conversations I had with President Hinckley over the years, I believe that President Stephen L. Richards was one of the giants in his life. As a young Church employee, President Hinckley quickly became a protégé of President Richards and he was obviously partial to him.

I remember that President Hinckley once characterized President Richards as the "best head" he had ever known. He was intelligent, wise, and careful. When faced with a difficulty, such as the problem with the draft deferments for missionaries, President Richards would often tell President Hinckley, "What we want to do is to compose the matter." According to President Hinckley, he was able to do this. He said one of the finest compliments President Richards ever received was a letter from U.S. General Lewis Blaine Hershey, which said, in effect, that if everyone dealing with his department had been as cooperative and reasonable as had the LDS Church, that his life would have been much simpler.

The philosophy of "composing" difficulties rather than fighting a bitter fight became almost a motto with President Hinckley. Over the years I often saw him transfer this principle into action. In this, President Hinckley was simply applying the remedy he had learned from President Richards of trying to "compose" differences and avoiding litigation.

"I WANT TO SEE HOW YOU DO IT"

Another exemplar in President Hinckley's life was President Henry D. Moyle of the First Presidency. President Moyle was in charge of missionary work while President Hinckley served as an Assistant to the Twelve. Once President Moyle asked Elder Hinckley how he gave instructions to missionaries and mission leaders. He explained that he taught how to find, to teach, to convert, to baptize, and to fellowship investigators. President Moyle said, "I want to see how you do it." So the two of them toured a mission together in California. Thereafter, they went out together to most of the missions in the United States, each discussing portions of these subjects. From this developed a very close relationship.

So close was President Hinckley to President Moyle, that he wrote a biography. of James H. Moyle, President Moyle's father, who had personally interviewed David Whitmer and recorded the personal testimony which David Whitmer bore to him of the visitation of the Angel Moroni.

"The Strong Influence He Exerted in the Highest Councils of the Church"

I had no personal contact with Gordon B. Hinckley between 1942, when I met him in the mission home in Salt Lake City, and April 9, 1970, when I met him again in the Upper Room of the Salt Lake Temple at the weekly Thursday meeting of the Council of the First Presidency and the Quorum of the Twelve. That was the day I received the unexpected call by the First Presidency to serve as the secretary to the First Presidency. On that occasion, I was introduced to Elder Hinckley—and all the members of the Council—by President Harold B. Lee.

I have no recollection about anything special that happened that day when I shook hands with him. It was not long afterward, however, that I became acutely aware of him and of the strong influence he exerted in the highest councils of the Church. I found that his voice was heard there more often and more persuasively than any other member of the Twelve. I infer the self-confidence that emboldened a junior member of the Twelve to do this traces from these main sources: First, President Hinckley seemed to have been endowed inherently with a supreme self-confidence. He never seemed to have been at a loss as to the course of action he or the Church ought to take in any given situation. Nor was he ever at a loss for well-chosen and apt words to express his thoughts, which always was done in good temper and spirits. And second, he was unusually well trained scholastically and in Church doctrine and procedure. As a young missionary, he literally sat at the feet of two Apostles, and observed their work and ministry day by day. Then, after his mission, he was asked by the First Presidency to fill a key role at Church headquarters, ultimately spending three quarters of a century in the inner circles of influence of the Church.

"He used the Talmage Room as his office"

In the early 1980s, two solemn assemblies were held on the fifth floor assembly room of the Salt Lake Temple for local priesthood leaders in the Salt Lake City area. As we prepared for those special events, President Hinckley asked me to accompany him to the temple to inspect the great fifth floor assembly room, where the special meetings were to be held. As the two of us walked through the upper floors of the temple, President Hinckley shared with me some very interesting experiences from his personal history.

He told me that it was on the fifth floor of the temple that the first film presentation of the temple endowment was prepared in the 1950s. President Hinckley was the one who oversaw the day-to-day work on this special project. He took great pleasure in showing me the places (on the north side of the assembly room) where the screen was set up as the backdrop for the filming, and where the cameras were placed (which were hoisted by cranes to the fifth floor, where they were brought into the building through one of the great round windows). He then showed me the rooms east of the assembly room where files and other documents were kept during the filming.

President Hinckley told me that he used the "Talmage Room" (the small chamber in the temple where Elder James E. Talmage wrote his *magnum opus*, *Jesus the Christ*) as his office. President Hinckley then showed me two other rooms beneath the Talmage Room, on two different levels. These two rooms are of approximately the same size as the Talmage Room. One of these two rooms had been sealed up for many decades until it was "discovered" by workmen in the temple in the 1950s.

As President Hinckley showed me around, I was amazed by the beauty and dignity that characterize these rooms, which have no present use and which stand bare and unoccupied. The décor is marked by the same beauty and careful workmanship that are seen in the other rooms of the temple that are regularly occupied and used. The master builders who constructed it obviously felt that "The House of the Lord" should be perfect from basement to attic, and the builders spared no effort or expense in making it so.

It was a source of great interest to me to observe the sense of excitement and pride in President Hinckley as he led me on a tour of these seldom-seen rooms. And he was anxious to explain to me the arrangement of the furnishings and equipment used in the planning and execution stages of producing the first temple ordinance film.

As this project unfolded, President Hinckley was brought into intimate contact with President McKay, and that exposure likely was influential in his call as an Assistant to the Twelve in 1958.

President Hinckley pointed out to me the location of one work desk he used, located behind the screen on the north side of the Assembly Room, where President McKay would often confer with him when he came to the temple to inspect the progress of the work.

President Hinckley told me that he continued to work directly with President McKay in preparing the first film presentation of the temple endowment. When the film was completed, President Hinckley personally carried it to Switzerland for use in the Bern Temple, which was dedicated in September 1955. He was not a General Authority at the time. This was the first temple built in Europe and the first temple to use the film presentation. Significantly, as a counselor in the First Presidency, he rededicated this temple in October 1992.

"The True Test of His Articulate Supremacy"

Among President Gordon B. Hinckley's many talents, his persuasive eloquence stands above all others. During my career, I have heard many eloquent men and women, but none to excel Gordon B. Hinckley. It has always been my personal belief that he was the most eloquent and effective speaker among all the General Authorities of his generation. His conference talks prepared in advance were always models of eloquence. But to me, the true test of his articulate supremacy was seen in the extemporaneous talks I heard him give in in a multitude of other settings, including area and stake conferences, administrative meetings, and in conversations in small groups. These impromptu sermons were on a variety of subjects that arose out of the discussions of the moment, so they were wholly unplanned on his part. On these occasions, the words came out as if played from an internal tape. They came out in complete sentences, each word seeming to have been carefully chosen to fit in its proper place. And the words were not ornate and abstruse, but were simple, plain words anyone could understand. But it was not the words alone and the carefully crafted sentences that made his speech so effective and memorable. His manner of delivery added to the impact. It was measured and reasonable, never strident or impassioned, and spoken with a sense of supreme self-confidence. Nor did he ever have to pause in search of a word. The precise word needed for the moment always seemed to be there ready to be spoken. I believe this was not an entirely learned skill but that much of it was an inheritance from father, Bryant S. Hinckley, who was also a most eloquent speaker.

"Impelled by a talk which President Hinckley had given"

During the administration of President Spencer W. Kimball, I witnessed the fruits of President Hinckley's powerful and persuasive eloquence. President Kimball came to my office one afternoon, bearing thirty-one one hundred dollar bills, which the Prophet had received from an anonymous donor in the mail. There was a letter of explanation with the cash. It had come from a conscience-smitten member who had committed some act of dishonesty and was impelled by a talk which President Hinckley had given in general conference about honesty, and who wanted to atone for some real or fancied sin of omission or commission.

"PRESIDENT HINCKLEY UNDERWENT A GRUELING DEPOSITION"

One of my first impressions of President Hinckley was his kindness. He was one man I would choose, were I given the choice, to sit in judgment upon my blackest sins. He was forgiving, merciful, charitable, and kind. He was also prayerful in the face of adversity. I often heard him pray that our hearts and the hearts of our enemies would be softened.

I observed these qualities in President Hinckley early in my association with him in the early 1970s. At the time, President Hinckley was involved in a lawsuit being litigated in Federal District Court involving the question whether the military deferment of our young men to serve missions was unlawful. In connection with this lawsuit, President Hinckley underwent a grueling deposition. Before attending the deposition, President Hinckley requested that the Brethren engage in a special fast and prayer, to the end that his mind would be enlightened and that the hearts of his adversaries would be softened toward him. After this event he expressed thanks to the Brethren and expressed the conviction that their faith and prayers were felt and had great effect.

"A RECURRING PHENOMENON IN CHURCH HISTORY"

President Hinckley exerted great influence upon all the Presidents of the Church with whom he worked. Each of the Prophets that President Hinckley served under and with whom I also worked with personally—Joseph Fielding Smith, Harold B. Lee, Spencer W. Kimball, Ezra Taft Benson, and Howard W. Hunter—had great confidence in him. An example of this confidence was demonstrated shortly before the Church's sesquicentennial in 1980. While final plans were being laid for the various celebrations that were to take place, I was sitting one day with President Spencer W. Kimball while he had a discussion with President Hinckley and President Boyd K. Packer about Church history. The comment was made that, at various times, great persecutions had arisen and almost overwhelming pressures exerted against the Church. President Hinckley then said that this was a recurring phenomenon in Church history and always would be. President Packer then made the comment that "the bells of hell" always ring when the saints set about to build temples.

Not long after this conversation, President Kimball asked me to write down for him my recollection of the conversation, as he wanted to use some of President Hinckley's thoughts in preparing his own talk and the dedicatory prayer to be delivered April 6 at the dedication of the new chapel at Fayette, New York.

"A HIGHLY DEVELOPED SENSE OF HUMOR"

President Gordon B. Hinckley had a highly developed sense of humor. President Hinckley once told me this story about a certain local leader of the Church. This man and his wife were very hospitable to leaders of the Church who visited the saints in their community and provided lodging for the General Authorities, but both were also noted for their unorthodoxy. President Hinckley told me that when he had stayed overnight in their home, the wife had pointed to the closet in the bedroom and said, "You can hang your clothes in there." Later, in the evening, when President Hinckley opened the closet door he found there were no hangers.

On another occasion, President Hinckley received a particularly aggravating letter, which he read to me. In the letter, the writer pulled out all the stops in criticizing President Hinckley for his service in the First Presidency and offered a list of suggestions on how he could improve. After reading me this letter, President Hinckley told me this story: He said that U.S. President Theodore Roosevelt once received a letter from a woman who asked, "President Roosevelt, is it true that as you charged up San Juan Hill you shouted at the top of your voice, "Damn it, damn it!" In answering the woman, Teddy Roosevelt said, "Madam. I don't remember what I said as I charged up San Juan Hill, but I do remember what I said when I read your letter."

"THE DECISION TO SELL THEIR HOME"

President Hinckley lived for many years in East Millcreek, where he had a large property with many trees. It was from one of these trees, planted decades before by the Prophet, that the new pulpit in the great Conference Center was constructed. There in East Millcreek, President Hinckley learned his first lessons of administrative leadership in the Church, ultimately serving as the stake president. The Hinckleys remained in the old family home up until the time President Hinckley was called as a counselor in the First Presidency.

As his duties in the first Presidency weighed down on President Hinckley, he sought living arrangements, which would ease his burdens and provide the peace and privacy that he and Sister Hinckley needed. He often spoke to me about his thoughts on finding a new home, commenting particularly about the unrelenting need for doing yard work at the old place.

One morning President Hinckley came to visit me in my office and told me that he and

Sister Hinckley had reached the decision to sell their home and to move into a condominium. He was growing very weary of the problems of yard work, snow removal, and security at his home. With my help, he began to look at condominiums in downtown Salt Lake City, including one on the penthouse floor of the Canyon Road Towers, where Helen and I lived, which contained over 3,000 square feet comprised of two units that had been consolidated into one.

Ultimately, however, President Hinckley decided to move into the then-recently-constructed Governor's Plaza Condominiums on South Temple Street. The Hinckleys remained there until he became President of the Church several years later. Not only was he greatly relieved to be done with snow shoveling and lawn mowing, but it was convenient for him to be only a few minutes away from President Kimball—and later Presidents Benson and Hunter—and from his office at Church headquarters.

"A PLACE UNIQUE IN THE HISTORY OF THE CHURCH"

In 1981 President Hinckley was called as an additional counselor in the First Presidency. Within a fairly short time following his call, the other three members of the First Presidency, Presidents Spencer W. Kimball, N. Eldon Tanner, and Marion G. Romney, were beset with a multitude of physical problems as the result of their advanced age. Following President Tanner's death in 1982, President Romney became the first counselor and President Hinckley the second counselor in the First Presidency. From that point forward until the death of President Kimball, President Hinckley was the only member of the First Presidency who carried out the day-to-day work of the First Presidency. Presidents Kimball and Romney were largely confined to their homes and unable to come to the office, except on rare occasions. That is not to say that they were not aware of and directly involved in leading out in the work. President Kimball still held the keys and was consulted on every major decision. But President

Hinckley really carried the lonely burden of leading out in the work on a day-to-day basis.

A few months after President Tanner's death, at a time when he was the sole healthy and active member of the First Presidency, President Gordon B. Hinckley shared with me a special spiritual experience he had received. He told me that he had been feeling the burden placed upon him, and indeed that he felt oppressed by the weight of his responsibilities. In this circumstance, he implored God for help and in answer received a powerful witness of the Spirit and the whispered assurance, "Be still and know that I am God."

President Hinckley then occupied a place unique in the history of the Church. He was, for all purposes, directing the Church. He had good help from the Twelve and other General Authorities. And, because of the long time he had been at Church headquarters (since 1935, with two years away during the war), he had a clear understanding about all aspects of headquarters administration. And it was my privilege and blessing to be at President Hinckley's elbow, as it were, during these lonely years when he alone stood at the helm of the ship.

"YOU BRETHREN GO FORWARD WITH THE WORK"

In the late 1970s and early 1980s there were several significant events that pointed toward the eventual calling of President Gordon B. Hinckley as an additional counselor in the First Presidency.

The first hint of the need for such a call came in about 1979, when after a long day of meetings, President Spencer W. Kimball expressed a deep weariness. I remember that he turned to President Tanner and President Romney and said, in essence, "I am done. I am finished. I can't talk. I can't write. I can't think. It seems that everything is arrayed against me. You brethren go forward with the work. I will try not to get in your way."

As he talked, tears came to the Prophet's eyes. His personal secretary, D. Arthur Haycock, who was with us, told me later he had never seen the Prophet cry before. He seemed so forlorn, so vulnerable, so disconsolate.

A day or two later, President Marion G. Romney came to speak with me. He said that he had received what he called "spiritual stirrings" of late that some new crisis was about to break upon us. He also expressed great concern about "three old men leading the Church."

President Kimball rallied again from this low point he experienced, but the ominous forebodings expressed by President Romney continued to unfold into reality.

"I'M JUST ABOUT AT THE END OF THE ROAD"

At the end of the 1970s and into the early 1980s, the three members of the First Presidency, Presidents Spencer W. Kimball, N. Eldon Tanner, and Marion G. Romney, continued to gradually decline in physical health. Old age was simply catching up with them, and they were becoming unhinged physically.

I remember one especially sweet and private conversation I had with the Prophet, not long before President Hinckley's fortuitous call to the First Presidency. One morning following a slate of meetings, President Kimball lingered behind, seeming to want to talk with me alone. After giving me a fatherly kiss, he said rather disconsolately: "Frank, I'm just about at the end of the road. I know the counselors don't like to hear me say that, but it is so."

As the months passed, more ominous signs of physical decline emerged. In early 1980 President Tanner's health took a serious turn for the worse. His eyesight was failing rapidly, and his doctors told him that there was little hope that he would ever be able to see well again. He had peripheral vision, but could not identify someone sitting directly across the table from him. Nor could he read, which was a significant handicap that greatly impaired his ability to direct the work. Acutely aware of this, President Tanner raised the question whether he should be released from the presidency and given emeritus status. This led him to mention in private conversation, or rather to imply, the possibility of calling a new counselor to the First Presidency. However, having spoken this thought out loud, he rejected this idea almost the moment he advanced it.

Within a few weeks, President Tanner was practically blind. He told me one morning that his eye doctor had told him that he had "reached the end of the road" as far as any hope of recovery was concerned. He confided in me that he felt incapable of assuming more responsibility than he already had, and that he did not feel "on top" of his work. He then again mentioned the possibility of suggesting to the Prophet that an additional counselor or counselors in the First Presidency be called, or even of beginning to use the members of the Twelve in that role, though unofficially.

About the same time as President Tanner was dealing with his advancing blindness, I one day walked with President Kimball to his office, giving him an arm to lean upon. As I left the Prophet at his door, he turned to me, saying, "You see the difficult situation we are in."

"THE TWO OCTOGENARIANS THEN WENT RACING DOWN THE TUNNEL"

In 1980 and 1981 the Church began gradually to face administrative problems arising from the fragile condition of the health of all three members of the First Presidency. Up until that point, the three brethren, Presidents Spencer W. Kimball, N. Eldon Tanner, and Marion G. Romney, were strong in mind and body. For example, I recall walking to the temple one day in about 1979 with President Tanner. As we walked, President Romney suddenly drew alongside.

"Why don't you lead the way?" President Tanner said to President Romney. At that, President Romney accelerated his speed into what was almost a run—and President Tanner picked up his pace to stay even with him. These two octogenarians then went racing down the tunnel toward the south entrance to the temple, as frisky as young colts. It was one of the most charming sights I carry in my memory, especially because of President Tanner's crouching, skimming walk. God bless the memory of these three giants—Spencer W. Kimball, N. Eldon Tanner, and Marion G.

Romney, who carried heavy administrative burdens of the Kingdom into their high old age.

"POISE AND ADROITNESS"

It was evident to me that President Spencer W. Kimball had perfect trust and confidence in President Hinckley even before his call to the First Presidency in July of 1981. In the months preceding his call, President Gordon B. Hinckley was repeatedly called upon to assist President Kimball and his counselors. Thus, during the Rochester Area Conference in April of 1980, Elder Hinckley accompanied the Prophet. Because President Hinckley could not see well, Elder Hinckley sat behind the President on the stand with a copy of his script in hand. Several times during the course of the meeting, Elder Hinckley prompted the President when he seemed to be having difficulty reading the teleprompter, thus saving him great public embarrassment. Then, at the October 1980 general conference, when three or four women in the balcony shouted, "No!" during the sustaining voice, Elder Bruce R. McConkie stood up and said that their vote had been noted, and that they should see Elder Gordon B. Hinckley. And, in March of 1981, Elder Hinckley joined President Kimball in paying a courtesy call on

President Ronald Reagan in the White House in Washington, D.C. These and other sensitive and crucial assignments he handled with poise and adroitness, making him invaluable to the ailing Presidency.

President Gordon B. Hinckley's call as a member of the First Presidency in July of 1981 was not a surprise to his Brethren in the leading councils of the Church. They were aware of his distinguished family background, of his wide experience in Church affairs, and of his unusual verbal and diplomatic skills. When the call had been extended, there was general recognition of the appropriateness of the call. He came to his new position well prepared in every sense. He had been intimately acquainted with the operation of the Church at headquarters for over forty years. For almost half that period he had been a member of the Twelve. His work as the Chairman of the Boards of the *Deseret News* and Bonneville International and as the Chairman of the Special Affairs Committee had given him special insights that would be invaluable to the Prophet. He had good judgment and was, in my estimation, by far the most eloquent of all the Brethren. The Lord had surely raised him up for this work.

At the meeting on July 23, 1981, when President Hinckley was set apart as a counselor to President Kimball, Elder Neal A. Maxwell was also ordained an Apostle and was set apart as a member of the Quorum of the Twelve Apostles, thus filling the vacancy in the Twelve created by Elder Hinckley's call.

"The Dominant Administrator in the Church"

President Gordon B. Hinckley served as a counselor in the First Presidency under President Spencer W. Kimball from the time of his setting apart on July 23, 1981, until President Kimball's death on November 5, 1985. During the intervening four years and four months he served as the dominant administrator in the Church.

His service under President Kimball can be divided into three general periods. First, the forty-one day period from the time of his setting apart on July 23, 1981, until President Kimball's major head surgery on September 3, 1981. During this time period, President Kimball was quite active and strong, and though Presidents Tanner and Romney were beset with a myriad of physical problems, the First Presidency operated with four members. Second, the period from September 3, 1981, until the death of N. Eldon Tanner on November 27, 1982. During this period, President Kimball's condition was extremely weak, and he seldom took any active role in Church administration. President Tanner was in a serious decline, but was about to rouse himself to active leadership. President Romney's condition was poor during this period. Third, the period from President Tanner's death on November 27, 1982, until the death of President Kimball more than three years later on November 5, 1985. During this final period, President Hinckley was essentially the lone man at the wheel, and except for a handful of major decisions and actions that President Kimball was able to participate in, President Hinckley essentially directed the Church under broad delegations of authority from President Kimball.

Never before nor since, in the long history of the Church, has there been a time when such a heavy burden rested upon the shoulders of one man. The only comparable period of time might have been from the fall of 1838 until the spring of 1839, when the Prophet Joseph was incarcerated in the Liberty Jail. Surely the Lord raised up Gordon B. Hinckley to serve in this significant role, which, in turn, prepared him for his own service as the sixteenth President of the Church.

"A COUNSELOR *IN* THE FIRST PRESIDENCY"

Not long after President Hinckley was called as President Spencer W. Kimball's counselor, I received a phone call from Roy Doxey, one of the editors of the *Church News*. He was calling to tell me that an article would be appearing in the next issue of the *Church News* about the new change in the First Presidency. He said that the reporters and editors at the *News* had been discussing the proper nomenclature to refer to President Hinckley's new position, and that the consensus was that President Hinckley would be serving as a counselor *to* the First Presidency rather than as a counselor *in* the First Presidency.

I raised the question with President Kimball, and he told me to look into the history and brief him on what had been done under previous Presidents of the Church in the unusual circumstance of calling more than two counselors. I knew that additional counselors had been called during the administrations of Presidents Brigham Young and David O. McKay. In the days of President

Young, the extra counselor was set apart as a counselor *to* the First Presidency, but later, during the administration of President McKay, his extra counselors were sustained as counselors *in* the First Presidency. I gathered all the evidence available on the issue for the consideration of President Kimball. He then decided that President Hinckley would be sustained as a counselor *in* the First Presidency.

When I advised Roy Doxey at the *Church News*, he was surprised—and I think a little disappointed. His view—a view shared by many—was that the revelation provides that the First Presidency consists of only three high priests and that if others are called to counsel with them, they really counsel that body which is already filled to capacity.

For all practical purposes, the different terminology was without significant distinction. Whether he served as a counselor *in* or *to* the First Presidency, President Hinckley still filled the same role.

"THE PROVIDENTIAL TIMING OF PRESIDENT HINCKLEY'S CALL"

Only six weeks after President Hinckley's call to the First Presidency, President Kimball faced one of the most significant medical crises of his life. A brain scan revealed an accumulation of scar tissue and blood beneath the membrane covering his brain. He was admitted to the hospital for major surgery. The surgeons removed a four-inch square section of his skull in the right front portion of his head near the eye. The offending matter was then removed through the membrane and the section of the skull cut out to allow the operation was wired back in place.

It was a major medical procedure, and the prognosis for President Kimball was very uncertain. The Prophet remained in intensive care for two or three days and then stayed in the hospital for another two or three weeks.

President Gordon B. Hinckley faced a daunting task. Though he lived for more than four years, President Kimball was never really the same following his September 1981 surgery. Nor were Presidents Tanner and Romney up to shouldering the heavy load of the Presidency. With general conference and the dedication of the Jordan River Temple looming, as well as a list of other meetings, conferences, and councils, and the usual crush of administrative business, President Hinckley certainly had his work cut out for him in the coming months and years. And he was surely up to the task.

Each day I became more and more impressed with the providential call of President Hinckley to the First Presidency, coming as it did at such a crucial time. President Kimball was almost completely incapacitated following his September 1981 surgery, attending meetings only sporadically. President Tanner was almost blind and heavily dependent on his secretaries, Dee Anderson and Larue Sneff. And President Romney struggled with poor eyesight, forgetfulness, and an increasing lack of self confidence caused by his physical disabilities and loneliness from the loss of his beloved wife, Ida.

The introduction into this group of three great, aged Prophets of a vigorous, able, and experienced younger man of only seventy-two had a remarkable effect on the administration of the Church. President Hinckley's hand was greatly strengthened by the uniform respect and confidence he received from the other members of the First Presidency and from the Twelve. It was indeed the hour and the day of President Gordon B. Hinckley.

"I WISHED THAT MORONI HAD A HOWITZER INSTEAD OF A HORN"

One of the most pressing tasks facing President Kimball's counselors as the Prophet lay in the hospital following his September 4, 1981 surgery was the dedication of the Jordan River Temple. President Kimball had broken ground on the structure on June 9, 1979, and by September of 1981 the temple was ready for the open house and dedication. Because President Hinckley was the only physically active member of the First Presidency, the brunt of the preparations and carrying out of the open house and temple dedication fell on his shoulders.

At the cornerstone laying ceremony, a news helicopter from Salt Lake City's Channel 2 flew over the audience several times in order to get good pictures for the evening telecast. The noise practically drowned out the remarks of President Hinckley who was speaking at the time.

Later, we received a telephone call from the director of news at Channel 2. He apologized profusely for the noise of the helicopter and said that the news staff was very embarrassed. In apologizing, the news director said, "At the time, I wished that Moroni had a howitzer instead of a horn."

"A MIRACLE OF THE FIRST MAGNITUDE"

Within days of President Kimball's September head surgery in early September of 1981, there was great pessimism expressed by his doctors and others about his chances of survival. Indeed, as general conference approached, the consensus of nearly everyone was that President Kimball would not survive until conference, and that he surely would never again be able to lead out in guiding the Church.

There were others, however, who believed that President Kimball would survive. Chief among them was President Gordon B. Hinckley. He had great faith that not only would President Kimball survive, but that he would "stand again before the people."

I recall being with Presidents Tanner and Hinckley shortly before the start of general conference in 1981. President Tanner raised the question of what the counselors should do were President Kimball to pass away before or during the coming general conference. President Hinckley was uncharacteristically quiet during this discussion. Then he spoke up and said, "I just have the feeling that President Kimball is going to get well."

President Kimball was unable to attend that conference, but President Hinckley continued to express confidence in the Prophet's recovery. He would often pray during meetings, with apparent conviction and faith that President Kimball would again be allowed to "stand before the people."

By March of 1982, President Kimball's physical condition was, if anything, worse than ever before. His eyesight and hearing continued to deteriorate; he was using a brace intermittently for his weakened back; his voice continued to weaken and to become more whispery; and his equilibrium became more shaky, and he occasionally fell as he tried to walk around his apartment. However, the Prophet seemed determined to attend the coming general conference, and, if he had his way, to speak at it.

On the Sunday of general conference in April of 1982, we all beheld a miracle of the first magnitude in fulfillment of President Hinckley's repeated prayers. President Kimball stood at the pulpit of the Tabernacle at the end of the afternoon session and bore his testimony and blessed the people. I never thought it would happen.

I will admit that I was among those who doubted that the Prophet would ever again stand and speak before the saints in a general conference. Shortly after his head surgery, President Hinckley began to pray in the meetings of the First Presidency that the Prophet would be allowed "to stand before the people again as Thy Prophet." On several occasions when he uttered these words, the thought came to me that he was asking the impossible. Moreover, I had the feeling that it was unfair to pray in such a way because of the great travail through which the President would have to pass in order to achieve it. But now that it was an accomplished fact, one had to acknowledge the rightness of it as demonstrating the power of faith and prayer in a most dramatic and convincing way.

"THE CHECKED EVERYTHING BUT MY I.Q."

President Gordon B. Hinckley was briefly hospitalized in May of 1982, which was a source of great concern to those at Church headquarters, since the Church could ill-afford to lose its only truly active member of the First Presidency. Given the weakened condition of the other members of the First Presidency, President Hinckley's illness could not have come at a worse time. And this fact was obviously weighing very heavily on the patient. His positive injunction to his doctor was, "Get me out of here as soon as possible."

He had been suffering from a lingering high fever due to an infection, and his doctor felt that he should be hospitalized in order to get the problem under control. He apparently had a similar attack several years previously during the dedication of the Washington Temple. Arthur Haycock told me that we almost lost him at that time.

President Romney and I went to the LDS Hospital to visit President Hinckley. He told us that it was the first time in his life he had ever been in a hospital as a patient. That was quite a record considering the fact that he was then in his early seventies. When we asked President Hinckley how he was doing, he told us about the multitude of tests the doctors were running on him, and then said, "They checked everything but my I.Q."

Gratefully, President Hinckley was soon healed and back on the job. Such a heavy burden rested upon him.

"PRESIDENT HINCKLEY WAS NOT AFRAID TO MOVE FORWARD"

There was almost no aspect of the work President Hinckley did not carry forward in the months and years following his call to the First Presidency in July of 1981. He installed new temple presidents, he trained new mission presidents, he traveled to Nauvoo to dedicate a number of newly restored homes, he traveled to the Far East to break ground for temples in the Philippines and in Taiwan, and he greeted political officials and foreign dignitaries to Church headquarters.

President Hinckley was not afraid to move forward with administrative changes. For example, he approved the completion of the placing of hundreds of satellite dishes outside stake centers in North America, which allowed special broadcasts to be viewed by members and Church leaders.

"NO SHRINKING VIOLET"

Following his surprising and providential call, President Gordon B. Hinckley lost no time in magnifying his new calling as a counselor *in* the First Presidency under President Spencer W. Kimball. Immediately after his call, I briefed President Hinckley about procedures in the Office of the First Presidency, and then I suggested that President Hinckley move into the office I had been occupying on the southeast corner of the first floor of the Church Administration Building. President Hinckley readily agreed, and I, in turn moved upstairs to the second floor.

Within a very few days after his calling, it was evident that President Hinckley's voice in the Presidency would be the dominant one. President Kimball appeared to have complete confidence in him. The fact that President Hinckley had been at Church headquarters for nearly a half a century, from 1935 until his calling in 1980, that he was blessed with great intelligence and judgment, that he had two decades of tenure in the Twelve, and that he was no shrinking violet in taking necessary action—all of this gave his comments powerful weight and influence. And the fact that he just came from the Twelve gave President Hinckley great status and rapport with that body, even beyond that of the other two counselors in the First Presidency.

"HE ALWAYS STAYED WITHIN THE BOUNDS OF HIS AUTHORITY"

Although he was alone at the helm for much of the time in the succeeding years, I observed that President Hinckley was very careful to never overstep the bounds of his authority. He always conferred with President Kimball on key initiatives and always deferred to the Prophet. And even though President Kimball's other two counselors, Presidents N. Eldon Tanner and Marion G. Romney, were suffering from the weaknesses of old age, President Hinckley always deferred to them, as well. President Hinckley, of course, began at that time to exert a dominant influence in the carrying out of the work of the First Presidency. Indeed, as a practical matter it could be said that Gordon B. Hinckley directed the Church for several years before the death of President Kimball. But, he always stayed within the bounds of his delegated authority. He never took action that plowed new ground unless he had the express authority of the Prophet.

"ANOTHER MARK OF PRESIDENT TANNER'S GREATNESS"

President Hinckley's influence was quickly felt at every level of Church administration after his call. His voice was heard most often and most persuasively in the meetings of the First Presidency and with the Twelve. Almost overnight he became the member of the First Presidency to whom everyone turned for counsel and direction in practically all things pertaining to Church governance. Only a few days before the surprising call in July of 1981, President N. Eldon Tanner filled that role. But because of President Tanner's weakened condition, his blindness and the ravages of old age, he seemed willing and pleased to yield that role to Gordon B. Hinckley. This was another mark of President Tanner's greatness—that he willingly took a more senior, advisory role and relinquished the role of chief leadership to the younger and more vigorous man.

"HE WAS WALKING A VERY TIGHT ROPE"

President Hinckley's task in serving as a third counselor in the First Presidency required a great measure of discretion and balance. He was walking a very tight rope. During this time period, I asked him how he was holding up, and he told me, "I live from day to day." The difficulty lay in the need for President Hinckley to keep the ship afloat, yet to do it in such a sensitive, skillful way as not to infringe on the authority and prerogatives of the aged men who outranked him in the First Presidency. I would rate him a grade of "A plus" for the way in which he performed under these difficult circumstances.

"The Situation Had Never Existed Before"

Not long before the death of President N. Eldon Tanner, President Gordon B. Hinckley came to my office to discuss a couple of matters. While he was there he seemed to be in the mood to talk and discussed a variety of subjects about his responsibilities in the First Presidency. It was apparent to me that he felt the full weight of the responsibility that rested on him. He mentioned how difficult it was to avoid overstepping his bounds when the senior members of the First Presidency were ailing. When I likened his situation to President Lee's while President Joseph Fielding Smith was alive, he observed, "Yes, but he was the first counselor." President Hinckley then commented that it was providential that President Kimball made broad delegations of authority to his counselors before he had his major surgery in September of 1981. He then commented that the organization of the Church was set up in such a way that almost any difficulty could be surmounted. President Hinckley pointed to Doctrine and Covenants 90:6:

>And again, verily I say unto thy brethren [the counselors in the First Presidency], . . . they are accounted as equal with thee in holding the keys of this last kingdom.

By virtue of the keys they hold, the counselors in the First Presidency have full authority to move forward with the work, despite the illness or even the disability of a President.

Shortly after I had this long conversation with President Hinckley, all of the older members of the First Presidency were afflicted with medical problems, which kept them from attending the regular meetings. President Tanner suffered a severe hemorrhaging of the nose, and President Kimball was also unwell and absent, as was President Romney. This was the first of many occasions over the next four years when President Hinckley was the only member of the First Presidency present at a presidency meeting. On this first occasion, however, it was a novelty, and I'm sure President Hinckley felt very alone.

Before the meeting began, President Hinckley visited with me and mentioned that the pattern of having an aged President in office likely will be perpetuated into the foreseeable future. I commented that the situation had never existed before which then existed, with the President and his first and second counselors being very infirm—and that this situation would not likely occur again. President Hinckley responded by saying that the answer would appear to lie in the President of the Church reaching down to call younger men to serve as his counselors and to release them promptly when it is seen that their effectiveness was impaired.

"I NOW BEGIN TO SEE WHY THE CATHOLIC CHURCH CREATED THE OFFICE OF ARCHBISHOP."

From an early period during his service as a counselor to President Spencer W. Kimball, President Hinckley had been impressed with the need to decentralize the administration of the Church. I recall that a few months after he joined the First Presidency, I had a long conversation with him about the great challenges facing the Church, brought about in large part because of the unprecedented and explosive growth of the Church that had occurred in the previous decade or two. President Hinckley then made this interesting observation—he said, in essence, "I now begin to see why the Catholic Church created the office of Archbishop." As we discussed this further, it became apparent that President Hinckley had in mind the idea that members of the Twelve, say five at a time, would be placed in charge of large areas of the world, under broad delegations of authority and responsibility from the First Presidency, to direct the affairs of the Church in these areas. Under this concept, two members of the

Seventy would be assigned to act as counselors to each member of the Twelve. These reflections were prompted by the special insights President Hinckley had received during the early months of his service in First Presidency, as he witnessed the bureaucratic structure that had been created at Church headquarters and the complications that existed at home and out in the world.

As he discussed these ideas with President Kimball and members of the Twelve in the succeeding months and they were prayed about and pondered, the Brethren were inspired to divide the international world into areas and to domicile three General Authorities in each area with authority to direct the Church there, subject to the overall direction of the apostolic leaders in Salt Lake City. However, it was decided that these area presidencies would be comprised of members of the Seventy, not members of the Twelve, who would remain in Salt Lake City and have worldwide jurisdiction over the Area Presidencies.

President Hinckley was the chief architect for two key organizational changes implemented at this time. The first was the creation of three executive councils chaired by members of the Twelve, and the second the creation of Area Presidencies with three General Authorities in each presidency, living the year around in the area served.

An integral part of this change was to give the Area Presidencies jurisdiction over all ecclesiastical and temporal affairs in that area. Until that time there was a split jurisdiction between what was called executive administrators and the directors of temporal affairs who were answerable to the presiding Bishopric.

This organizational set-up positioned the Church to expand globally in an efficient, concerted way, dividing the areas as the work requires it. It provided for decentralization by giving the Area Presidencies wide discretion, while giving adequate overall control by the hierarchy through other administrative mechanisms, which President Hinckley was chiefly responsible for implementing.

Under this control mechanism, three headquarters executive Councils were created—Priesthood, Missionary, and Family History and Temples. Each Council was comprised of three members of the Twelve, two presidents of the Seventy, and a member of the Presiding Bishopric. The senior member of the Twelve on a council was the chairman. In addition to having authority over the headquarters departments falling under it, each executive council had authority and responsibility for a third of the areas around the world. Thus, President Hinckley envisioned that each Area Presidency would go to the executive council under which it fell for direction and advice. Actually, the headquarters contact man for an Area Presidency was the chairman of the executive council. Should the executive council be unable to respond, the matter could be taken to the Twelve for handling and ultimately to the First Presidency, if necessary. Because members of the Executive Councils would be in regular sometimes daily contact with their area presidencies and because Area Presidencies would be in regular contact with stake and mission presidents through stake and district conferences and mission tours, as well as through correspondence and telephone communications, President Hinckley believed the Church would be able to move forward as an integrated whole on a worldwide basis. The fact that members of the Seventy have apostolic authority, which enables them to set in order the affairs of the Church in their respective areas, provides the necessary flexibility and discretion so that local problems can be solved in a special, tailored way. And the Area Presidencies receive regular instruction from members of the Twelve during area, regional, and general conferences to insure that governing, apostolic standards are met. As already indicated, such an organization will make it possible to continue the accelerated growth of the Church worldwide through the increase of seventies and new areas as the work requires.

These proposals resulted in the establishment of areas in the Church, presided over by Area Presidencies, a major dismantling of the huge bureaucracy at Church headquarters and a major reassignment of duties to the Presiding Bishopric of the Church.

In retrospect, the contribution of President Hinckley in the implementation of these changes is Providential. These changes essentially equipped the Church to deal with almost unlimited growth in the future.

"Broad delegations of authority to President Hinckley"

With the death of President Tanner and with the new and heavy responsibilities given to him, President Hinckley entered into a new important phase of his training as a future President of the Church. President Hinckley's duties increased dramatically after President Tanner's death. Shortly after his death, President Kimball called President Romney as his first counselor and President Hinckley as his second counselor.

President Romney, aware of his own advanced age and exhibiting great humility and unselfishness, suggested several times to President Kimball that Gordon B. Hinckley be called as the first counselor. President Kimball resisted this noble suggestion, but it is a mark of the greatness of Marion G. Romney.

President Kimball set apart President Romney as his first counselor, and President Romney set apart President Hinckley as the second counselor. Shortly thereafter, broad delegations of authority to President Hinckley were given by both President Kimball and

President Romney. They essentially authorized him to act on behalf of the First Presidency in all matters pertaining to Church governance. This really made Gordon B. Hinckley the de facto President of the Church. Notwithstanding his authority to act, President Hinckley, however, was extremely deferential to President Kimball and always consulted with him before breaking any new ground or moving forward on significant callings or initiatives. In many respects, the following three years were the finest hour, not only for President Hinckley, but for Presidents Kimball and Romney as well. All three were great men and true stalwarts of the restored gospel.

In the early days after President Tanner's death, President Hinckley was not alone in the council meetings. President Kimball and President Romney frequently attended, most often in wheelchairs. President Kimball contributed to the discussion and made all the ultimate decisions. This was truly inspiring to see, as it was clear that notwithstanding his physical limitations, President Kimball was still at the helm.

"President Hinckley still bore a heavy burden"

In the early months after President Tanner's death, President Hinckley made the wise decision to enlist the more active assistance of the Twelve, and President Ezra Taft Benson in particular, in handling the heavy load of the work. For example, President Hinckley decided that he would ask President Benson to conduct the opening and closing sessions of the general conference and to speak at the general priesthood meeting and the Sunday morning general session. It was decided that President Hinckley would make a brief statement at the beginning of the Saturday morning session, turning the conducting over to President Benson. Even with President Benson's able assistance, President Hinckley still bore a heavy burden at this and succeeding conferences.

"One of our greatest Presidents"

My regular interaction with President Gordon B. Hinckley ceased following my release from the Seventy in 1991, and thus I have little personal knowledge of the events surrounding his service after that date. However, having spent much of two decades in close proximity to him, including a period of nearly five years of almost daily interaction, I think I am qualified to offer some insights about his character, his contributions, and his legacy for the Church.

It is difficult to assess the relative strength and greatness of the Presidents of the Church—in fact it is impossible to do so. The Lord raises up His servants to serve during specific times. Each brings his own unique qualities, which are perfect for his generation. However, in examining the broad sweep of Latter-day Saint history, it is possible to see some giants standing in the long shadow of history. President Gordon B. Hinckley is surely one of these. He is undoubtedly one of our greatest Presidents. Born into one of the great families of the Church, he was chosen almost in his youth for conspicuous service at Church headquarters. For a period of nearly seventy-five years, he worked closely with the highest leaders of the Church, first as a staff employee, then as a General Authority, then as a member of the Twelve, and finally for a period of several decades as a member of the First Presidency.

As with every leader, he faced unique challenges. One of the greatest tests of his character and leadership occurred during the final five years of President Spencer W. Kimball's administration, when President Hinckley was the only physically active member of the First Presidency. This was a circumstance that never before nor since has occurred in Church history. During those years, most of the meetings of the First Presidency included President Hinckley alone, with me taking minutes. I can testify that he was magnified greatly during that period and was under the constant guidance of heaven. It was during that difficult time that President Hinckley began to envision administrative solutions to problems that had dogged the Church for many years. Those problems arose primarily from the explosive growth of the Church. President Hinckley had the vision to see long-term solutions to those problems, which outfitted the Church for almost unlimited growth in the future. He harnessed the revealed structure of the priesthood in a way that set the Church on a firm and certain course. In all of this, President Hinckley was the architect, acting under the delegated authority of President Kimball.

On a personal level, we have rarely seen a more eloquent President of the Church. President Hinckley at the pulpit was inspiring, enlightening, almost poetic. He spoke best, it seemed, when he spoke extemporaneously. In private settings he was, if possible, even more eloquent, moving people to tears, inspiring change in individuals and organizations.

As one who spent many years literally at President Hinckley's elbow, I can testify that he was truly a Prophet of God.

ABOUT THE AUTHOR

Daniel Bay Gibbons is a writer living in Holladay, Utah. The youngest son of Francis M. Gibbons and Helen Bay Gibbons, he is a former trial attorney and judge and is the author of several previous books. He has served as a full-time missionary, twice as a bishop, and as president of the Russia Novosibirsk Mission.

INDEX

Made in the USA
Charleston, SC
01 January 2017